Computer Love

Theresa Cox

DEDICATION

I dedicate this book to my Lord and Savior
Jesus Christ!
He is the head of my life, and I thank him
for making me unique and truthful. Even
when the truth hurts sometimes, I try to keep
it all the way honest about this game called
life. It's not easy but it is worth it!

CONTENTS

Dedication   iii

Table of Contents   V

Introduction   7

The Sex Machine   17

The Ryder   29

The Great Pretender   50

Computer Love or War   63

INTRODUCTION

Computer love is love at a fast pace, lightspeed, with little to no time to get to know a person. It's a love that doesn't need much courtship and real-time for getting to know each other. Computer love can be based on lies or truths; depends on how desperate you are for love. Loving on a computer with few conversations can lead to adventures of finding the right one or murder.

Computer love is supposed to make finding love easier, faster, and accurate; only if you put every personal detail in plain view for people to see. You are supposed to get the results of a great relationship after posting personal details about yourself. In most cases, it doesn't work because people choose to put every lie they can think of about themselves. The computer love season has made it easy for people who don't want anything but to mess your world up.

Easily with the touch of a button everything can change. Men who already have a wife who look for what she does not do or what they desire for, or single men who don't want to be married use the season of computer love to escape. What was supposed to be love to women, in return has brought us liars, cheaters, pedophiles, and users to get up close and personal with you and your families. Ladies tell your neighbor quick! The 2004 census said black women were the most single women in the United States. We tend to take pride in being the strongest women on the totem pole. When we have no intention of falling for a sorry dude; the enemy will prepare one or two or even twenty-five for us. It keeps repeating itself until we recognize what we are attracting or what's not right for us.

On weak days... yes, strong women have weak days too. Weak days are days full of being saved, but those particular days must be managed with care. I don't care how strong you are, you will fall for one that the enemy prepared for you. We still end up as single as the other side of the stick. Proverbs 18:22 states, "He who finds a wife finds a good thing and obtains favor from the lord."

The question is what types of men are finding you? If a man does not see a wife in you, what does he see? What types of men are attached to this computer love era? First off, I want to congratulate all women reading this book that wants a good man in their life. What does single women call a good catch or a good man? A good catch in the computer love era, is a man who is in the right place, breathes the right air, and say the right things. However, there are plenty of us still walking this beating path and waiting for Mr. Right. I have three types of men to avoid at all costs they are: The Sex Machine, The Great Pretender, and The Ryder.

The sooner you realize what attracts you the less heartache, pain, struggle, embarrassment, defeat, bitterness, and just plain madness you will be able to avoid. I've learned in the computer love era that using these smart devices has "slowed" us down. Our discernment of who the enemy is has dulled our senses. It has put us in denial and we still don't want to believe, as the song says, "This Is It." Make no mistakes where you are! The bible speaks of how we will go after unsound doctrine over the word of God, because of our itching ears. Our ears don't like the truth. I have been single for half of my adult life. I've been in the church even before my son was born and he is twenty-two years old. I have yet to meet a man in the church for me. Why? In the scripture of James 1:14 it states, "But every man is tempted when he is drawn away and enticed by his lust." In this computer love era, the mind tends to make up its agenda or games of love and sex. Church ladies have a sex game. OH YES, Church ladies have sex games they play too. Now don't get it twisted by chances you may find a man in the church. Women will use these games such as; we are going to date on the phone only, when I get a ring I'll give him all the premarital sex he wants, and finally I gave him some one time just to see if he knows what he is doing. He must marry me now. Instead of playing these games, we need to fall on our knees and pray.

Seek God and ask for his guidance. Playing these games will not guarantee marriage and matter of fact it guarantees you won't get married. Men love to play games as well. The answer yes to their questions can never be said. For example, he asks can he take you out to a dinner and a movie? Church girls should say no, but you can go to church with me on Sunday. Every television Evangelist became who he is because a girl, preacher, or someone in the church said NO! She wouldn't be a "beauty spot" either as my grandmother would say. That beauty spot knew not to show a lot of teeth or smile. She also knew to say no to everything he put out there. In this computer love era, men have mastered all types of agendas against us. I mentioned in the beginning the three types to

avoid. Now when we don't have any power,

self-esteem, drive, or energy left, here comes

a man who can find the last fiber of our

strength and pull on it and ruin our whole

world.

THE SEX MACHINE

The Sex Machines have a particular type too. Her name is Sister Minnie. She got saved when she was single and loved the Lord. Sister Minnie has one thing that most saved women have. They either hide it or just come out with it and that was Sister Minnie was sexy! She has always been attractive. She has lovely legs and a curvy soul sister shape! Sister Minnie has a bright smile with an attractive personality! She was sure of herself and spoke what was on her mind. She had every man in church cheesing when he saw her! The church ladies didn't like how she had her way with the men in church. Sister Minnie could get the men of the church to do whatever she asked. Some would call what she had a lust spirit. It was her anointing. She could not hide it. When she walked into the room. Women would grab their husband as if Sister Minnie wanted them. Those lame, purple suits, hen-pecked dudes! Sister Minnie was not desperate for anyone's man! She wanted her own man! Her type had to be single, tall, handsome, and good looking! He had to have his own successful business and his own home. He should be saved and love the lord. He had to have bedroom swag! Sister Minnie knew who had the swag and who did not. It was all in his handshake. He was not in the church at least not her church! She was not afraid of her sexiness. Oftentimes the enemy would prepare one just for her. She ran into guys who pretended to be whatever she needed them to be until they got what they wanted. You would think Sister Minnie would learn after a couple of imposters or sex machines, but this cycle kept going. Sister Minnie was hoping for a miracle that just won't come! At least, not the last time I saw her in church. She was just a saved hot tail woman like most with no knowledge and no relief. She was too shy to open up to the elders about her dilemma! Most hot tail women are afraid to be honest about themselves and their situation! This syndrome is called a hot tail woman. In the African American community, a "Hot Tail" is a woman who lusts after men and changes men like she changes underwear. If she is in church, a hot tail woman has never been told by anyone, "sweetie when you get saved you don't have sex anymore until you get married." Simply because everyone in the church have their own agenda. When it comes down to the secret sin called sex, if you are not sharp you will relapse repeatedly with who? you guessed it …

The Sex-Machine! Even more, the enemy never promised he would leave you alone. The sex machine and the hot tail woman of God should avoid each other at all costs. The Sex Machine might be the piano player who gets at least two hot tail women of God pregnant in the church. A hot tail is saved but never been delivered and just tried but can't help herself on her weak days. She needs a way to escape. A way of escape can last as long as twenty-four hours or as small as a body magic. A Body Magic is a girdle that fits tightly and can't easily be pulled down. Just in case the Sex Machine comes by on your weak day or night be strong. The Sex Machine don't care if its day or night if he wants to get your hot tail. He knows body magic by names and would touch you and ask, "why do you have on a body magic?" A weak day for a hot tail woman will have her frustrated and she will growl at everyone. You've been praying but nothing has given you relief. Cold showers can't even help you. You can't even bend over to get a piece of paper without thinking of a sex position.

The Lord already has revealed to you that the Sex Machine is no good for you. You know he is too good to be true! You started with the word of God on your brain. At this point, you are so horny your tail takes over your thoughts. On that hot day the Sex

Machine will say everything and be whoever it takes to get that body magic down and around your ankles. When he calls on your hottest day DON'T ANSWER THE PHONE. Lay down... no sit up and call an elder to pray for you. You can keep it honest with God but don't tell your praying partner what your illness is. That's between you and God! By chance if you let the Sex Machine in your presence you are no match for him. If you do happen to engage in sex with him, he will move on quicker than a fart on a gassy day. The Sex Machine will turn into anyone he needs to be to get your hot tail. He can be a husband for a little bit, but his burning desire for sex will lead him to cheat. He can be a boyfriend or a good stepfather to your children for a while, but he will soon become unavailable. They don't call him the Sex Machine for nothing, because he is great at what he does! He can even be a churchgoer for a season, but he can never be faithful for any reason. After he gets your hot tail you are no longer any good to him. It's all about the chase for him.

Now whether it's hereditary or you pick it

up in life you must gain control of your hot tail. It's okay, don't get mad, get better. Go to church and let the lady elders lay hands on your belly and cast that hot tail spirit out and let the holy spirit in. Especially, when that Sex Machine you thought was the one is now gone. The withdraws from the Sex Machine will almost make you lose your mind. You will be thinking to yourself if you had done it to him in a different position he would have stayed or came back. NO, NO, NO he would not. He will not come back unless you are a Sex Machine and he has met his match. When he meets his match, it will be time to reap what he has sown and that's only in God's timing.

Always remember that a Sex Machine can spot hot tails out a mile away. You might not even know you have a hot tail, but if you have been with five men in a year that means you have a hot tail. Nevertheless, submit yourself unto God. He is the only one who can wipe away your sins, so come to him in meekness. That means hand God your hot tail and stop snatching it back whenever a Sex Machine comes your way. I know what I'm talking about. You will be snatching it back from God and then you'll say, "I'll be right back."

In your mind every man has the potential to be a husband. Most likely it is a Sex Machine in sheep's clothing! When you snatch that hot tail back from God it's because you think you got something to do. When the cycle of the Sex Machine is over there is no one there but you and God. There is no one there to pick up the pieces of you off the ground. This is the road for the Sex Machine. On this road he is king and there is no stopping him.

THE RYDER

The Ryder is next on the computer love list.

The Ryder is smooth. He is the one who picks

up the intelligent successful women with

multiple college degrees. The Ryder may go

to college or he may not. He may work in fast

food or be a drug dealer. He sees you, but you

don't see him until he's all the way in. Before

you know it, he is driving your car with the

cellphone you got him. You will see Ryder is

a long-time hustler.

He saw you in high school and followed you right-through your college graduation. He can tell you everything about you and he knows who your best friends are. He makes sure he stays out of their view, until the wedding is planned and set. Terry has graduated from Emory University School of Law and has a great job waiting for her in Texas. Her mother struggled and worked three jobs to meet every financial deadline until she graduated. They were seeing the light at the end of the tunnel and Terry was excited. She was starting a new journey and her friends wanted to take her out to celebrate. Even though she didn't drink, she went with her friends to the local watering hole. They were having so much fun she didn't notice the man that was staring at her. Her friends got up and went to the bathroom. She sat at the table and waited. The handsome stranger came to the table and greeted her. "Hi Terry!" She looked at him with confusion. "Do I know you?" Terry asked. "We went to high school together I'm Will, Will Johnson." Will smiled. Terry told him she didn't remember him. He said he graduated a year before her and was now working as a Sanitation Engineer for the city. That means he is the trash man and has a small side hustle as well. He did not carry a long conversation. He asked for her number and walked away to continue enjoying his night. Terry did not speak on her encounter to her friends. They enjoyed the rest of their night joking and laughing about life. As time pressed on Terry was settled into her new job as partner at a great firm. She started receiving calls from Will. He began to visit

Terry frequently. She was intrigued by him and the date was set! She was getting married in a month. Her friends and family didn't have a clue. He had quit his job in their hometown and had been in Texas for months. Terry always was a private person. When she came to visit family and friends, they were shocked she was marrying Will. They said things like, "you do know he got eight kids with eight different women." "He was the trash man and the weed man!" Terry didn't hear a word they said. It was as if she had cotton in her ears. She had bought him a

BMW when they were in their hometown to visit. He had dropped her off to her mother's house and she didn't see him anymore until it was time to go back to Texas. Her mother was furious. She hated him with a passion. That was supposed to had been her BMW, she thought to herself. All those years of struggling and now this. She began to question Terry's mental state. Terry said, "look mama I love Will." "No, he's not perfect, but he's perfect for me." Terry stated proudly. "Here is five hundred dollars, go and buy u something nice." "I don't want to hear anything else about Will being a sorry no good man, he's going to do better." "His children are coming in the summer and you can come for Christmas." Terry's mother was furious. How could Terry do her like this? All the overtime and prayers she prayed had gone to waste. She put in all that time and all she got was a five-hundred-dollar check! Terry's mother knew what type of man he was. He was sucking her daughter dry and she knew it. The wedding was in a month and he knew Terry's mother didn't have any love for him. He also knew he had Terry's nose wide open. When she went to the doctor and she was three weeks pregnant it was a wrap! He married Terry and the rest was history! He's been to Mexico, Hawaii and Canada. Any place you can think of he has been. He hasn't worked in a pie factory. Terry's mother just knew those trips were going to be for her and her daughter. Will made sure he blocked it all. The last we heard Will was going to truck driving school. He quit, because it hurt his foot when he held the brake pedal down! He is a Ryder! He can dress and act the part of a together man to fool most people. If your Ryder thinks he is smarter than you he will hide you and never marry you. The smartest Ryder is a man on a million-dollar status without even walking down the aisle. They're only a few who make it to this level, but they say few words and are seen very rarely. When a Ryder is dating you best believe there's something big in it for him or he's out of the relationship. If he leaves you best believe he is moving onto bigger and better opportunities in the next relationship. The only way you are going to find a Ryder doing bad is because he got caught up on drugs, and he still is going to have a woman working behind the scenes keeping him afloat. Imagine a pimp and a ho scenario except the ho has no idea she's being pimped out, because there's no common sense to see she is being tricked to death. He always carries a slick smile and in his mind all women fall for him and his slick ways.

When women don't fall for his slick ways, we have to be homosexual in his mind. He will then try to keep his woman away from any friends or family who threatens his Ryder ambitions. Her mother is definitely a threat.

She rarely gets to hang out with her mother, because mothers are one of those people next to God. You can fool some of the people most of the time, but you cannot fool God and most mothers none of the time. Her mother knew he was a Ryder from the first day he stepped on her porch. If a Ryder's woman or wife gets to spend time with family or friends, she has put her foot down. Today, when you put your foot down it means (you already made it clear what you are going to do and what you expect others to do). Each party has accepted their defeat in this matter for the sake of loving her.

Even though the Ryder doesn't give a "Beep" about you or what your family thinks. If by chance the scales fall off your eyes towards Ryder and you get a divorce Ryder doesn't want to pay child support. Remember you are the sole breadwinner of the relationship. You will end up paying him spousal support and child support to his outside of the marriage kids because looking back he never held down a job. He will always have several ideas and plans that his type will fund or try to help him accomplish.

As soon as he gets that job or that diploma

and you are about to take a sigh of relief, Ryder will find something wrong with that job and never go back. He may pretend that he is going back for several days or weeks. He will be over his boy's house until he finds the right time to tell his type he is not going back. At the end of the day he is a Ryder. Ryder got his ways from an overachiever single mother. Most likely who spoiled him to the bone, and she stills takes up for him. When Ryder has a problem at home, his mother will always agree with her son and take his side. She's like a steel trap door about her Ryder baby! Ryder has grown more than the Great Pretender or the Sex Machine in this season.

The Ryder will house all three of these characteristics. Living in the last days, there is such a lack of men who will not take their proper place in society. Women are becoming more independent. Women need men less but need them more. Isaiah 4:1 states, "And in that day seven women shall take hold of one man, saying, we will eat our own food and wear our own appeal: only let us be called by thy name, to take away our reproach." This means women can take care of themselves, but they need a man to give them their last name. It looks better with his name on it.

Independent, successful, women are biting like a fish on a hook. Not loving for the sake of love, but for the total package of marriage and what makes her look successful. In this case, the Ryder loves what it looks like to his friends and family. There are so many of these horrors. Women refuse to open their eyes to growth and more. Women in this situation assume loving is hard, when loving is easy. Ryder looks for his type who loves as a job, a hard job at that. I once saw a photograph of a woman who had her Ryder on her back, her husband or Ryder was dressed neatly in a suit and smiling with a big smile riding on her back. Her daughter was in her arms, the woman's face was wrinkled and looked stressed. Her clothes were fitted loose and outdated. The son was running behind. His shoes untied, and his clothes were in disarray. His eyes were staring deeply at his mother. She was looking ahead as to be unconcerned of nothing because all her focus was being drained out of her.

A Ryder's relationship tends to affect the physical and mental health of women. We weren't meant to carry the heavy load of the relationship. Genesis 2:18 "And the Lord God said, it is not good that the man should be alone; I will make him an help meet for him." Women are working nine to five, picking up groceries, cleaning, paying all the bills, taking kids to all the events, getting them ready for school, and to every doctor appointment. They are making sure the kids are at every practice and church function, while he sits and criticizes their every choice or decision. He just wants to keep her under his thumb and control.

When you approach a man first, you are saying you will accept the greater part of the relationship. As I stated before in Proverbs 18:22 it states, "He who finds a wife finds a good thing and obtains favor from the Lord." There is a saying called "Don't hustle backwards." My grandmother would say you hustling backwards when you approach a man. You are saying, Ryder doesn't have to change his cheating or selfish ways to be in the relationship. Guess what again, Ryder knows that, just like a lion does with its prey. His type has a degree, great career and stability outside the home, but you are less respected once you become attracted to Ryder.

The Ryder will continuously gaslight her. Google's definition of Gaslighting is a form of psychological manipulation and which a person or group convergingly sow seeds of doubt in a targeted individual. Making them question their own memory, perception or judgement. The Ryder is often evoking cognitive dissonance and other changes such as low self-esteem. Then the kids see their father always getting away with gaslighting the mother, so they do it as well. If you want to know if a man love you ask a child.

Ryders are the kings and queens of their castle because they refuse to give you the power or respect. You hardly see Ryder outside with his type of woman. Business dinners and award ceremonies that celebrate her he will miss. She will often make excuses for his absence unless she promises a gift of his liking. He will come with a sour demeanor to kill her high. Every so often we run across a flamboyant Ryder who wants everyone to see him being what he is a Ryder of all Ryders. She is whipped, clueless, and everyone sees what she doesn't see. He will dress immaculately and maybe be cute or not. He must outshine her at her event. He comes in with assurance that his game is working for him. Watch your coattail because these are the schemes of a Ryder.

THE GREAT PRETENDER

Last, but certainly not least GREAT PRETENDER. The Great Pretender is the worst of them all by pretending to love you. He will tell you he loves you all the time to ensure that his love bug has bitten you. He makes you feel like you can't live without him. You receive him with little to no knowledge of who he is.

He will have every woman in your life smitten. Mother, grandmother, and even your sisters too! He will always be welcome to your mother's house. Even after you have ended the relationship. He is still welcome, because he has the charm of a snake. No matter what you tell your family he did, they will say "He didn't mean it." "Give him one more chance, he was such a nice one you let get away."

He is the one dating every woman on the block and have every lady rolling her eyes at you for nothing. Until one day she's bold enough to knock on your door and say he has a disease and she is just letting you know. You are looking crazy because you weren't aware he was cheating, but you're not giving him sex. Who did you think he was getting it from? He is the type who will be cheating on you with your best friend. They are great liars and when it comes to the Great Pretender he can hurt you one or four different ways. The great pretender pretends to love you, but he hates the women he attracts. Do you know why? He makes sure he finds someone totally different from you and it will be someone he stated, that he would never date. He goes and treats her like a queen. The Great Pretender had you thinking that you were the only one he wanted. In the end, you don't know because his act was so well played. He could have five wives and you would never know.

In online dating, they are the horror stories that you hear about. Yes, that's him The Great Pretender. He is the kind of man who does everything right. He rubs your feet, shows up at your job with lunch, calls several times a day, always opening car doors, gives you money, and talks about marriage. He talks about marriage because he knows if you are a lady of God that's what you want to hear. The Great Pretender would have the ugliest woman thinking she is fine as wine and her head in the clouds. A songwriter had said, "Took me riding in a rocket and gave me a star, but a half-mile from heaven you dropped me back down unto this cold cruel world." This is the results from a Great Pretender. The only thing that can reveal what he is made of is time. A Pretender can't pretend forever. If you can hold out one or two months longer than him. Then you have done your heart a great justice. When he gets caught up he will not take the blame. It will always be your fault. When he sees your family at the mall, he will have a sad story of how he doesn't know why you broke it off with him. Guess what? They will believe him.

The woman who breaks him down in the end is a very sweet but not too attractive sister or straight up hood rat. These two different women make The Great Pretender change his ways or get in church. The sister from the hood knows his game and is like "Is he bothering you?" This is taking place in a grocery store, as he sparks up a conversation with the single lady just talking to see if he still has game. He secretly knows his hood rat would knock his head off his shoulders at any given moment. They move on down the aisle with a tap on his head and a loud fuss.

The sweet sister that you don't expect to change him, changes him completely. Let me introduce you to Tangela. Tangela is from the back side of Kentucky. Her home was off a long dirt road just her and her grandmother. She was always in church, a Holiness church to be exact. Tangela only knew Jesus Christ and country living. Her grandmother raised her up that way. She never wore make up or pants. She was a sweet southern girl who never had a perm! Grandma would put a hot comb through her hair every Sunday morning. She knew how to cook too. One day while in the kitchen cooking, Tangela heard a loud thump! She ran into the living room only to find grandma had a heart attack and died! After the funeral, Tangela's cousin on her father's side said, "Tangela come to Nashville Tennessee with me to stay." "There is no reason for you to stay here anymore!" "Grandma is gone!" Retha yelled. Tangela was not city savvy, but she trusted her cousin.

Grandma always told her the city was for FAST girls, but what did she have to lose? She sold the house and moved to Nashville. Tangela was wondering was she making the right decision. Everything in Nashville was moving way faster than what she was use too. She was trying to make the best of the change in her life. Tangela's cousin Retha got her a job at the front counter of the coffee shop near the community center. Tangela was not the cutest girl in Nashville, but everyone talked about how nice and sweet she was. One day this fast talker with a bright smile came in and ordered some coffee. Tangela took his order and served him up a cup of Java. For some reason Tangela did not like his loud flashy ways, and how he knew everyone except her. He came in everyday at the same time and ordered the same thing. Finally, he introduced himself as Mr. Charles Daniels. He worked down the street at the bar as a bartender. He also ran a card house as well. She knew he was a worldly man, very handsome, tall, well dressed, and always had that slick smile. One day Mr. Charles Daniels said, "hello" and Tangela asked, "can I help you?" Like always, Tangela was displaying her holiness. She wanted him to know she was saved and has been anointed. You know the kind, long skirts and long ponytails who don't show their teeth to any men. Grandma taught her to not show her teeth to men. When you smile at men they think you want something. Mr. Charles Daniels came around every day and finally got the nerve to ask could he take her out to dinner? She said no at least fifty times. Then finally she told him he could go to church with her one Friday night. The Holy Ghost filled the service.

Charles was a church guy. He was used to the bar and his card house all night making big money, but every time he asked her to dinner she would say no and offer him a visit to church. The more he went the better he felt. One Sunday Tangela had her eyes closed and the pastor was giving the call to Christ. She felt Charles get up and the rest is history! He is now the Pastor of Don't Stop Get it Get it Tabernacle. This is where Tangela is the SMILING First Lady! For the sweet lady that is so sweet she breaks the Great Pretender right down. She is so sweet he can't even run his game on her because he feels guilty. She takes him to church and now he is your pastor because he knows how to adapt to all people. Remember he was a great pretender before he got saved. Always remember that the Great Pretender gets a thrill talking about his past accomplishments in the game of love. Never be a pawn in his game. Hold out and trust your gut and wait for God to expose him for the Great Pretender he is.

COMPUTER LOVE OR WAR

In closing I was once told, "A man changes for one woman." So just maybe when you're out with friends or at the hardware store you might be eyed and approached. One that is willing to change his Sex Machine, Ryder, and Great Pretender ways for you. My grandmother always said, "It's a bad wind that never changes." Another saying that means your ways will catch up with you and only if it doesn't make you change. You are bad and there is no cure for what you do. If you are one of these men or women, know to find yourself and then request an order of change through Christ Jesus. He is the only way to true love because he is love. The Bible tells us in Hebrews 12:2 "Looking unto Jesus the author and finisher of our faith; who for the joy that is set before him endured the cross, despising the shame and is set down at the right-hand of the throne of God." This verse means he knew your life wouldn't be easy and there would be troubling times. Even despising some shame now and then for you. He already knows your life, like a book that has been read. No matter what you go through, he is seated in a place of favor and encouragement for you always. You are going to meet some people who are not going to mean you any good. You might even be that guy who hurts a lot of women, but God will forgive you and change you into a better person. Therefore, you will go and do right towards all. Ladies, I know it's not easy being alone or sometimes played like a football playbook. I know you are tired of the plays, but with God on your side, YOU ARE GOING TO WIN.

Just be obedient to God's plan and you shall have the desires of your heart. Prayer and living a holy life will keep the Sex Machine, Ryder, and the Great Pretender out of your life. A reformed man of one of these types you won't be able to keep him away. He will see God in you. Be blessed and know men know what you're going to be to them when they meet you and if it's not a wife then make him out of a lie.

www.ingramcontent.com/pod-product-compliance
Lightning Source LLC
LaVergne TN
LVHW011338080426
835513LV00006B/425